The Pocket Prayer Book for Soldiers

Battlefield Prayers in Times of Need

Sandra E. Henderson, M.Ed.

Copyright © 2014 by Sandra E. Henderson, M.Ed.

The Pocket Prayer Book for Soldiers
Battlefield Prayers in Times of Need
by Sandra E. Henderson, M.Ed.

Printed in the United States of America

ISBN 9781628717471

All rights reserved solely by the author. The author guarantees all contents are original and do not infringe upon the legal rights of any other person or work. No part of this book may be reproduced in any form without the permission of the author. The views expressed in this book are not necessarily those of the publisher.

Unless otherwise indicated, Bible quotations are taken from The Nelson Study Bible. Copyright © 1997 by Thomas Nelson, Inc.

www.xulonpress.com

PRAYERS

I.	Prayer of Salvation.	11
II.	Prayer for When I am Lonely.	12
III.	Prayer for When I am Fearful.	13
IV.	Prayer for When I Need to be Comforted .	14
V.	Prayer Before Engaging in Battle	15
VI.	Prayer for those in Authority	16
VII.	Prayer for When I Need God's Protection .	17
VIII.	Prayer for my Fellow Soldiers	18
IX.	Prayer for my Family	19
X.	Prayer for God's Guidance.	20
XI.	Prayer of Thanksgiving and Praise to God.	21
XII.	Prayer in time of Grief and Pain.	22

Introduction

The Prayers in this book are short, to the point and based on God's Word. They can be prayed at any time and are short enough for you to memorize and hide them in your heart. There is Deliverance in God's Word. May God our Holy and righteous Father richly bless you and bring you safely back home to your loved ones. Praise God!

Foreword

This prayer book is powerful! The prayers and scriptures were inspired by God and penned by my mother, author Sandra E. Henderson, in 2003 over the course of 7 days. God led her to write this small but mighty prayer book that can 1) be taken anywhere, including the battlefield, 2) be used to offer comfort and 3) bring Glory to God. She feels a deep connection to military men and women all over the world who selflessly sacrifice so much to protect and serve others. Surrounded by military men in her family growing up, she understands the importance of encouragement, spiritual support, prayer and the power of God that is evoked when we pray God's word, and come to Him in our Savior's name. She has been a believer all her life and is definitely known as a Prayer Warrior. To her, that means being on the frontline and interceding for her family and others every single day without fail. Like many of you, she is a warrior. She is my prayer warrior and it is an honor that God has shared the power of prayer through her, with me and now to soldiers all over the world. God bless you as you read, pray and carry this book.

[Signed]
Tiffany N. Dennis

I. Prayer of Salvation

My Decision to Receive Christ

I admit that I am a sinner, because Your Word says that we all have sinned and fallen short of the glory of God (Romans 3:23). I want to repent and turn away from my sinful life (1 John 1:9).

I believe that Jesus Christ died for me, [*Your Name*] on the cross (1 Peter 2:24). This day/night I invite You into my life. I want to follow You and I do trust You. I now, at this moment accept You as my Lord and Savior. In Jesus' Holy name, Amen. (John 1:12, John 3:16)

_____

Date I Received Christ

II. Prayer for When I am Lonely

God,

Your Word tells me that You will never leave me or forsake me and that You will be with me always and even until the end of the age. Father, I thank You for being with me now. I am strong and I know that my strength comes from You. Thank You for being the one who goes with me. I am seeking to feel Your presence and I thank You for being with me and I know that I am never alone.

In Jesus's name, Amen.

(Hebrews 13:5, Matthew 28:20)

III. Prayer for When I am Fearful

Lord God,

Right now I am fearful about [*Fill in blank with your own words*] . I pray that You will take all fear away from my mind. Father, Your Word says You have not given me a spirit of fear, but of power and love and a sound mind. Therefore I put my fear away and receive power from You oh God, to help me. I refuse to be bound in fear, because I know that Your Word says that You will give Your angels charge over me to keep me in all my ways. I am reminded that although I walk through the valley of the shadow of death I will fear no evil because God, Your rod and staff bring me comfort. Thank You for Your assurance that in You there is no fear. In Jesus' name, Amen.

(2 Timothy 1:7, Psalm 91:11, Psalm 23:4)

IV. Prayer for When I Need to be Comforted

Father,

God of all comfort, I need to be comforted now. I thank You for Your Holy Spirit, which is the Comforter. Lord, Your Word says that You comfort us in all our tribulations, so that we are able to comfort others who are in any trouble, with the comfort with which we are comforted by You God. Almighty God I thank You for the comfort and peace that You have given me. Father I pray, please help me to comfort others just as You are comforting me. Thank You. In Jesus' name, Amen.

(2 Corinthians 1:1-5)

V. Prayer Before Engaging in Battle

God,

As we go into battle I thank You for Your protection. I know that there is nothing or no one that can protect me, only You Father. Your Word says that if I obey Your voice and do all that You speak, then You will be an enemy to my enemies and an adversary to my adversaries. Lord, I submit to You now. Thank You Father because I know that You, God go before me and will fight for me. I know that the battle is Yours. Yeah though I walk through the valley of the shadow of death I will fear no evil for You are with me. Your rod and staff, they comfort me. Thank You for Your provision in the midst of this battle. I plead the blood of Jesus now, in Jesus' name, Amen.

(Deuteronomy 1:30, Psalm 23:4)

VI. Prayer for those in Authority

Father God,

I come to You, giving You glory and honor. I bring those that are in authority before You now. Lord I pray that You, through Your commandments will make them wiser than our enemies although they are ever with us, Lord, I thank You that our plans are established by counsel; and by wise counsel is war waged. I pray that we will be divinely directed by those in charge. I pray that they will call upon Your name and seek Your will. I pray for their protection from the evil one. This is for the Commander-in-chief on down. I thank You, in Jesus' name, Amen.

(Psalm 119:98, Proverbs 20:18)

VII. Prayer for When I Need God's Protection

Father,

I thank You for Your protection from all hurt, harm or danger. Lord I put my trust in You. I thank You for Your Word as I pray it back to You. You say that Your Word will not return to You void. I pray Father, that no weapon formed against me shall prosper, and every tongue which rises up against me in judgment, You shall condemn. Lord this is the heritage of the servants of You Lord and any righteousness is from You Lord. Thank You for Your angels, which encamp around me. Thank You for establishing me and guarding me from the evil one. In Jesus' name, Amen.

(Isaiah 54:17, 2 Thessalonians 3:3)

VIII. Prayer for my Fellow Soldiers

Dear Lord, May Your glory continue to abound. God, I lift up my fellow colleagues to You at this time as they have left their families and friends to come together to share their skills and talents in this battle. I ask for Your divine protection for them now. I thank You for using them in the manifestation of Your glory. Please bless them and give them courage and strength in these uncertain times. I pray that each and every one of them will seek You as their savior and that Your peace will abound in them. I pray that they will put on the whole armor of You God, so that they will be able to stand against the wiles of the devil. Thank You Father for each of them as we bond together as family for a common cause.

In Jesus' name, Amen.

(Ephesians 6:12)

IX. Prayer for my Family

Father,

In the Name of Jesus, I thank You and praise You. Thank You for my family as I bring them before Your throne. Father, Thank You for Your protection of my family. I bring [*Fill in blank with your own names*] before You now and ask that Your glory be manifested in their life now. Since I am not able to be physically present, I ask that Your Holy Spirit will comfort them in my absence. Calm their fears and meet their needs according to Your riches in glory by Christ Jesus. Although I miss them, I know that since they are in Your hands, no evil shall befall them, nor shall any plague come near their dwelling; for You have given Your angels charge over them to keep them in all Their ways. Thank You heavenly Father,

In Jesus' name, Amen.

(Philippians 4:19, Psalm 91:10-11)

X. Prayer for God's Guidance

Dear God,

Glory and honor be Yours alone. Lord today I ask for Your guidance as I go about my day. Please lead me and guide me with Your eye as Your Word says. Please help me to know the way in which I should walk. Help me to say and do as You would have me. I thank You for Your help. My special need at this time is

[*Fill in the blanks with your own words*] . Thank You Father for Your loving kindness and it is in You that I trust.

In Jesus' name, Amen.

(Psalm 143:8)

XI. Prayer of Thanksgiving and Praise to God

Father,

Your Word tells me that it is good to give You thanks and praise Your Holy Name. You are worthy to be praised. Father Your Word declares that You have done marvelous things, and I thank You for all that You have done. I especially thank You for the presence of Your Holy Spirit and [*Fill in blanks with your own words*]. Once again, I am thankful to You God and Bless Your Name.

In Jesus' name, Amen.

(Psalm 92:1, 95:2, 100:4)

XII. Prayer in Time of Grief and Pain

Heavenly Father,

Praise be unto You. I come at this time with a heavy heart because I am grieving and I'm in pain. Lord, I thank You for consoling me. I pray that You will comfort me in all my tribulations so that I will be able to comfort those who are in any trouble, with the comfort with which I am comforted by You God. Lord, as I mourn, Your Word says thank You for having mercy on my affliction. God, Your Word says that You do not want me to be ignorant, concerning those who have fallen asleep, lest I sorrow as others who have no hope. Lord You say that If I believe that Jesus died and rose again, even God will bring with Him those who sleep in Jesus. With this in mind, I know I will see them again. Thank You Father because I know that Your Word will not return to You void.

In Jesus' name, Amen.

XII. Prayer in time of Grief and Pain

(2 Corinthians 1:4, Matthew 5:4, Isaiah 49:13, 1st Thessalonians 4:13)

www.ingramcontent.com/pod-product-compliance
Ingram Content Group UK Ltd.
Pitfield, Milton Keynes, MK11 3LW, UK
UKHW022211230426
12048UKWH00016BA/779